Free Gift

I want to say Thank You for buy~~~~ ~~~~ ~~~~ ~~ ~ put together a free gift for you!

"Bonus Recipes to checkout"

This gifts is the perfect compliment to this book so just hit the link below to get access

Click Here to Download Your Free Gift.

Tom Soule Collection

Table of Content

Free Gift 1

Table of Content 2

Introduction 4

The Paleo Diet Explained 5

The Do's 7

The Don't's 9

Bring On the Slow Cooker 11

Benefits of Slow Cooking 14

Recipes 16

Breakfast 17

Breakfast Casserole Meaty Medley Slow Cooker style 18

Lunch 20

Cauliflower Bolognese slower cooker paleo 21

Traditional Squash Soup Paleo style 22

Ginger Butternut Squash slower cooker 24

Apple Cider Spice Butternut slower cooker.................................. 25

Thai Curry slower cooker Paleo style... 26

Bacon Jalapeno Paleo style... 27

Dinner.. 28

Paleo Sausage Stuffed Peppers Paleo style 29

Slow Cooker Beef Stroganoff spicy... 31

Seasoned slow cooked Veggies 33

Cheesy Paleo-Style Tortillas 34

Lemony Chicken Slow cooker style 36

Honey Glazed Chicken Wings 37

Honey Glazed Drumstick Medley...38

Sweet Potato Chicken Mash slow cooked 39

Thai Curry Chicken 40

Orange Flavored Chicken Paleo style..41

Sweet Treats 42

Maple Gazed Pecans Slow Cooked..43

Stuffed Apple coconut cream slow cooked 44

Conclusion 46

Free Gift 47

Reference...48

Introduction

If you are looking for a book that provides you with a "get-ripped-quick" scheme or a "lose ten pounds with these ten meals" method, this is not the book for you; however, if you are looking for a book to enhance your overall health, transform your eating habits, and add some delicious recipes to your collection, you have come to the right place!

Take another look at the title. Do you notice something missing? Nowhere in the title does the word "diet" show up. The same can be said for the rest of the book. While the word itself means the type of food a person eats, the negative connotations of the word often lead people astray; we don't want any confusion when it comes to the paleo lifestyle. Think of paleo not as a diet, but as a way of life.

This book will cover what paleo is all about, how to utilize a slow cooker in this lifestyle, and amazing recipes that will add some oomph to your new dining experience. Without further ado, let's get started!

The Paleo Diet Explained

What Is The Paleo Lifestyle? (Yesterday and Today)

In order to understand a lifestyle, it's important to know the history behind it. The Paleolithic style of eating began thousands of years ago (sometimes people call it the "caveman diet"). Early humans mainly ate meat, fish, vegetables, and fruits to sustain themselves. Many of these principles are seen in the modern version of the lifestyle, including the exclusion of dairy, grain, and processed foods. Many people believe it's a healthier lifestyle option.

In the past, people didn't simply choose to eat this way; rather they adapted to their environments and lived off the land. The common categorization for their communities revolved around the hunter-gatherer lifestyle. They often ate what was readily available to them and whatever could be gathered in abundance.

Today, there are several methods of achieving this lifestyle due to the variety of foods available to us. Some people choose to commit to the "old-fashioned" sense of the paleo lifestyle in terms of what they will and will not eat, but you should choose the level of commitment that works best for you.

Now that you have the basic historical understanding, we will move on to the common do's and don't's.

The Do's and Don't's of Paleo

All lifestyles comes with certain rules or conditions, and the paleo lifestyle is no exception. By following the rules, you're ensuring that you'll actually see the results you want (remember: these rules are there for a reason). At the same time, these rules aren't entirely absolute. Everyone is different and will look to alter the list as desired, so never feel as though you cannot do the same. The purpose of this book, once again, is to help you decipher the best way to fit "paleo" into your life.

The Do's

Here is a list of food items that are recommended as part of this lifestyle:

- **_Grass-Fed Meats_** – These particular animals are raised in cruelty-free environments and eat grass, hay, and other wild plants. <u>Common meats</u>: beef, pork, lamb, veal, rabbit, goat, sheep, chicken, turkey, etc.
- **_Fish and Seafood_** – <u>Common seafood</u>: salmon, tuna, trout, bass, halibut, sole, tilapia, cod, crab, lobster, shrimps, scallops, clams, oysters, etc.
- **_Fresh Fruits and Vegetables_** – <u>Common fruits</u>: bananas, apples, oranges, berries, grapefruit, pears, peaches, nectarines, plums, pomegranates, pineapple, papaya, grapes, etc.<u>Common vegetables</u>: celery, tomatoes, bell peppers, onions, leeks, kohlrabi, green onions, eggplants, cauliflower, broccoli, asparagus, cucumber, cabbage,

brussel sprouts, artichokes, okra, avocados, lettuce, spinach, carrots, mushrooms, squash, etc.

- ***Eggs*** – <u>Common eggs</u>: chicken eggs, duck eggs, goose eggs, quail eggs, etc.
- ***Nuts and Seeds*** – <u>Common nuts and seeds</u>: pistachios, sunflower seeds, sesame seeds, pumpkin seeds, pecans, walnuts, pine nuts, macadamia nuts, chestnuts, cashews, almonds, hazelnuts, etc.
- ***Healthy Oils and Fats*** – <u>Common oils and fat</u>: avocado oil, olive oil, coconut oil, flaxseed oil, butter, clarified butter, duck fat, veal fat, lamb fat, nut butters, nut oils, coconut flesh, coconut milk, etc.

Remember that this list is only the beginning; several other food items fit into the paleo lifestyle. Just because you don't see your favorite foods on this list doesn't mean they won't work! These are just basics to help familiarize you with what you should eat.

The Don't's

Here is a list of food items that should be avoided in this lifestyle:

- **_Grains_** – <u>Common grains</u>: corn, rice, wheat, barley, rye, buckwheat, quinoa, etc.
- **_Legumes_** – <u>Common legumes</u>: peanuts, beans, peas, lentils, etc.
- **_Dairy_** – <u>Common Dairy</u>: milk, butter, cheese, ice cream, ghee, cream, etc.
- **_Refined Sugar_** - The terms sucrose, glucose, fructose, maltose dextrose, lactose, high fructose corn syrup, molasses, honey, evaporated cane juice, fruit juice concentrates, cane crystals, and corn sweetener all indicate the presence of these sugars.
- **_Potatoes_** – <u>Common potatoes</u>: russet, jewel yam, Japanese sweet potato, red gold, Yukon gold, etc.
- **_Processed Foods_** – These foods contain a collection of artificial ingredients that are not good for your body.

- ***Salt*** – <u>Common salts</u>: table salt, seasoning salt, sea salt, etc.

Again, some people may choose to still include some of these items in their daily meals; however, it's recommended that you avoid them (if possible).

Bring On the Slow Cooker

Now that we have all of these wonderful food items to work with, you may be scratching your head and asking, "What now?" The next step is the find an effective way to cook your food that is healthy, diverse, and, above all, simple. The solution: a slow cooker, popularly known as a Crock-Pot. You may have seen this appliance in your grandparents' home when you were younger or in the deep corners of your parents cabinets. Wherever you have seen it before, or if you own one already, get ready to break it out and give it a prominent role in your kitchen; it's about to become an important part of your new lifestyle!

What Is A Slow Cooker?

That is a great question! First, the technical answer: A slow cooker is an electrical appliance that is used for simmering foods on relatively low-temperatures. The simple answer: a slow cooker is an inexpensive countertop electric pot that allows you to cook dishes without attending to them at all over long spans of time. Sounds like a product worth having, huh?

Slow cookers are usually made out of ceramic or porcelain and are surrounded by a metal casing. The covering of the pot is normally made of glass and helps to keep in the vapor that is collected as the food cooks. This vapor level depends on how much water is added to your recipe. A majority of cookers present you with heat settings to properly assess the needed heat for your meal, but some have one temperature setting that gets the job done.

You can purchase a slow cooker from any store, online or otherwise, that sells kitchen appliances.

How It Works

Now that we have our slow cooker, it is time to plug it in and get cooking! We will go in depth with recipes later, but this is a brief overview of how it works:

1.   Place the cooker on a heat resistant surface; the bottom is known to get very hot.
2.   Add raw food and liquids into the cooker.
3.   Place the cooker's lid on securely and turn on your cooker.
4.   Select your heat setting. (Note: some cookers may alter the heat automatically after a certain amount of time has passed since the time it was turned on. Check your cooker's settings for more information).
5.   As the food begins to cook, the vapors within the pot will rise up to the lid and return

to the pot as a liquid. This process also takes place on the sides of the pot, which helps to distribute flavors.

6.   Leave the food cooking for the prescribed amount of time (this will depend on the particular recipe).

7.   After the needed time is complete, let your food cool down. Cookers are known to continue cooking food after they are turned off.

8.   <u>An extra tip</u>: using a cooker is great when you are making food to transport to another location because it often keeps the food hot and does not require it to be reheated once at the location.

And that's it! It does not get any simpler than this!

Benefits of Slow Cooking

Slow cooking is easy. Even so, you may still be wondering about all the buzz surrounding slow cooking. If you're not convinced of the usefulness of a slow cooker, check out this a list of the most notable benefits that come along with this cooking technique:

- A longer cooking time allows the flavors of your food to be distributed more evenly while really soaking into the food.
- Due to the low temperature, you're less likely to ruin your food by burning it or losing it to the bottom of a pan (what a cleaning nightmare)!
- The slow cooker will allow you to buy less expensive food items, such as tougher meats, because they are tenderized during the process.
- It is a one-stop-shop for cooking your meals, so you no longer have to slave over a hot stove with a watchful eye. The slow cooker practically does all the work for you! All you have to do is load it up.

•Lastly, it-is very convenient! When you walk away from your cooker, you know that your food is being prepared well and is a healthier alternative to the other methods of cooking.

Recipes

So now that you have the foods and the necessary tool, you need some meal options, right? Never fear! Here are some simple recipes from around the paleo eating community to help get you started.

Breakfast

These breakfast recipes will give you the kick-start you need to begin your day. Having a good breakfast is crucial in any lifestyle, as it gives you the energy to get through the day while decreasing the chances of unhealthy snacking.

Breakfast Casserole Meaty Medley Slow Cooker style

Prep Time: 30 minutes
Cook Time: 8 hours, 0 minutes
Total Time: 8 hours, 30 minutes
Servings: 4-6

Ingredients

- Softened ghee or palm shortening to grease slow cooker
- ½ lb. bulk breakfast sausage, crumbled
- 8 strips of bacon chopped
- 1 ½ lb. white sweet potatoes, peeled and diced
- 2 bell pepper diced
- 1 sweet pepper diced
- 18 large eggs, mix until completely yellow
- ¼ cup almond milk
- ½ cup full-fat coconut milk
- 1 teaspoon salt
- ¼ teaspoon black pepper
- 1 onions diced

Instructions

1. Grease slow cooker with softened ghee or palm shortening.

2. Cook sausage, bacon, and onion in a skillet over medium-high heat for 10 to 12 minutes, until the sausage is browned and the onion is softened. Drain off excess fat.

3. Place shredded sweet potatoes in the slow cooker and press them down slightly.

4.   Add meat and onion mixture and bell peppers to slow cooker.

5.   In a large bowl, whisk together the eggs, milk (almond and coconut), salt, mustard, and pepper. Pour into slow cooker.

6.   Cover and cook on low for 6 to 8 hours.

Lunch

After a long morning, the breakfast you had is going to be running a bit thin. Thank goodness it's time for lunch! A good lunch will fill you up and keep you going, no matter what the afternoon has in store for you. By keeping things paleo-style, you'll be eating healthy too!

Cauliflower Bolognese slower cooker paleo

Prep Time: 10 minutes
Cook Time: 3 hours, 30 minutes
Total Time: 3 hours, 40 minutes
Servings: 5-6

Ingredients
- For the bolognese:
- 1 head of cauliflower, cut into florets
- ¾ cup diced red onion
- 2 small garlic cloves, minced
- 2 teaspoons dried oregano flakes
- 1 teaspoon dried basil flakes
- 2 14oz cans diced tomatoes, no salt added
- ½ cup vegetable broth, low-sodium
- ¼ teaspoon red pepper flakes
- salt and pepper, to taste
- For the pasta:
- 5 large zucchinis, Blade A

Instructions
1.   Place all of the ingredients for the bolognese into crockpot. Cook over high heat for 3.5 hours.
2.   When done, smash the cauliflower with a potato masher or fork until the florets break up to create a "bolognese."
3.   Spoon the bolognese over bowls of zucchini noodles.

Traditional Squash Soup Paleo style

Prep Time: 8 minutes
Cook Time: 6 hours, 0 minutes
Total Time: 6 hours, 8 minutes
Servings: 4-8

Ingredients

- 1 large butternut squash (about 6 cups cubed)
- 1 can (14 ounces) coconut milk
- 2 cups of chicken stock
- 1 granny smith apple, peeled, cored, and cubed
- 2 carrots, peeled and chopped
- 1 teaspoon ground cinnamon
- 1 teaspoon ground nutmeg

Instructions

1. Cook all ingredients on low heat for 4 to 6 hours.

2. Blend or puree when cooking is finished. (An immersion blender is ideal for this. If you don't have one, let your mix cool before transferring it to a blender or food processor.)

3. Garnish with your choice of seasonings, including (but certainly not limited to) cinnamon, nutmeg, curry powder, pumpkin seeds, and bacon.

Ginger Butternut Squash slower cooker

Prep Time: 8 minutes
Cook Time: 6 hours, 0 minutes
Total Time: 6 hours, 8 minutes
Servings: 3-5

Ingredients

- 1 large butternut squash (about 6 cups cubed)
- 1 can (14 ounces) coconut milk
- 1 cup of chicken stock
- 6 carrots, peeled and chopped
- 1 cup of raw cashews, chopped
- 1″ piece of ginger, grated
- 2 teaspoon of ground cumin
- 2 teaspoon of ground cinnamon

Instructions

1. Cook all ingredients on low heat for 4 to 6 hours.
2. Blend or puree when cooking is finished. (An immersion blender is ideal for this. If you don't have one, let your mix cool before transferring it to a blender or food processor.)
3. Garnish with your choice of seasonings, including (but certainly not limited to) cinnamon, nutmeg, curry powder, pumpkin seeds, and bacon.

Apple Cider Spice Butternut slower cooker

Prep Time: 8 minutes
Cook Time: 6 hours, 0 minutes
Total Time: 6 hours, 8 minutes
Servings: 3-5

Instructions

- 1 large butternut squash (about 6 cups cubed)
- 1 can (14 ounces) coconut milk
- 2 cups apple cider
- 2 apples of your choice, peeled, cored, and cubed
- 1 carrot, peeled and chopped
- 1 teaspoon ground cinnamon.
- 1 teaspoon ground nutmeg.

Instructions

1. Cook all ingredients on low heat for 4 to 6 hours.
2. Blend or puree when cooking is finished. (An immersion blender is ideal for this. If you don't have one, let your mix cool before transferring it to a blender or food processor.)
3. Garnish with your choice of seasonings, including (but certainly not limited to) cinnamon, nutmeg, curry powder, pumpkin seeds, and bacon.

Thai Curry slower cooker Paleo style

Prep Time: 8 minutes
Cook Time: 6 hours, 0 minutes
Total Time: 6 hours, 8 minutes
Servings: 3-5

Instructions

- 1 large butternut squash (about 6 cups cubed)
- 1 can (14 ounces) coconut milk
- 2 cups chicken stock
- 2 carrots, peeled and chopped
- 2 heaping tablespoons of red curry paste
- 1 small red onion, chopped
- 1″ piece of ginger, grated
- 6 cloves of garlic, chopped

Instructions

1. Cook all ingredients on low heat for 4 to 6 hours.
2. Blend or puree when cooking is finished. (An immersion blender is ideal for this. If you don't have one, let your mix cool before transferring it to a blender or food processor.)
3. Garnish with your choice of seasonings, including (but certainly not limited to) cinnamon, nutmeg, curry powder, pumpkin seeds, and bacon.

Bacon Jalapeno Paleo style

Prep Time: 8 minutes
Cook Time: 6 hours, 0 minutes
Total Time: 6 hours, 8 minutes
Servings: 3-5

Ingredients
- 1 large butternut squash (about 6 cups cubed)
- 1 can (14 ounces) coconut milk
- 1 cup chicken stock
- 2 carrots, peeled and chopped
- 1 granny smith apple, peeled, cored, and cubed
- 2 jalapeno peppers, chopped. (Remove the seeds if you desire less heat)
- 6 ounces of crisped bacon, chopped
- 4 cloves of garlic, chopped

Instructions
1.   Cook all ingredients on low heat for 4 to 6 hours.
2.   Blend or puree when cooking is finished. (An immersion blender is ideal for this. If you don't have one, let your mix cool before transferring it to a blender or food processor.)
3.   Garnish with your choice of seasonings, including (but certainly not limited to) cinnamon, nutmeg, curry powder, pumpkin seeds, and bacon.

Dinner

After a busy day, you'll need a good dinner to help you make it until breakfast tomorrow. These paleo-friendly dinners will give you all the nutrients you need to get through the night. Of course, they also make use of your slow cooker, meaning you can start these before you leave your house in the morning and come home to a warm, home-cooked meal, all without very much effort.

Paleo Sausage Stuffed Peppers Paleo style

Prep Time: 35 minutes
Cook Time: 6 hours, 0 minutes
Total Time: 6 hours, 35 minutes
Servings: 3-5

Ingredients
- 1 pound of ground Italian hot sausage
- 5 bell peppers, assorted
- ½ head of cauliflower, grated or chopped into a "rice-like" consistency
- 1 small (8 ounce) can of tomato paste
- 1 small white onion, medium dice
- ½ head of garlic, minced
- 1 small handful of fresh basil, minced (or 2 teaspoons dried)
- 2 teaspoons dried oregano
- 2 teaspoons dried thyme

Instructions
1. Cut the tops off of your peppers and scoop out seeds (be sure to save the tops!).
2. Process or chop about half a head of cauliflower into "rice" and put in a large mixing bowl.
3. Add minced garlic, basil, and dried herbs, and onion to cauliflower and mix by hand.
4. Optional: Over high heat, use a skillet to lightly brown sausage (the sausage will cook just fine in your slow cooker, but browning it can bring out more flavor).

5.   Add sausage and tomato paste to seasoned cauliflower and mix by hand.

6.   Fit as much sausage mixture into peppers as possible. Place peppers into slow cooker and loosely place the pepper tops back on. If you have extra meat and cauliflower mixture, add it in between your peppers and let it cook.

7.   Cook on low for 6 hours.

Slow Cooker Beef Stroganoff spicy

Prep Time: 15 minutes
Cook Time: 4 hours, 30 minutes
Total Time: 4 hours, 45 minutes
Servings: 5-7

Ingredients

- 2 lbs. beef stew meat
- 2 teaspoons salt
- ½ teaspoon pepper
- 1 teaspoon garlic powder
- 2 teaspoons. paprika
- 1 teaspoon thyme
- 1 teaspoon onion powder
- 8 oz. sliced mushrooms
- ½ onion, sliced
- ½ cup coconut cream (scooped from the top of a refrigerated can of coconut milk)
- 2 teaspoons red wine vinegar

Instructions

1.	In a small bowl, mix together all spices. Place meat in a large bowl and sprinkle with the spice mix. Mix everything together using your hands, and coat the meat well with the seasoning.
2.	Place sliced mushrooms and onion in slow cooker. Lay seasoned beef on top. Put the lid on the slow cooker and cook on low for 4 1/2 hours.

3.   When the meat is tender and nearly done, add the coconut cream, vinegar, and any additional salt or pepper. Stir around and cook on high (with the lid ajar, if possible) for roughly another hour.

Seasoned slow cooked Veggies

Prep Time: 11 minutes
Cook Time: 3 hours, 0 minutes
Total Time: 3 hours, 11 minutes
Servings: 3-5

Ingredients

- 2 bell peppers, cut in large slices
- 1 large sweet potato, peeled and cut into cubes
- 3 small zucchinis, cut in thick slices
- ½ cup peeled garlic cloves
- ½ teaspoon salt
- 1 teaspoon Italian seasoning (or substitute your preferred seasoning)
- 2 tablespoons olive oil

Instructions

1. Grease slow cooker, then add all the veggies.
2. Season with the salt, seasoning, and oil, then stir to evenly coat.
3. Cook 3 hours on high (or longer on low), stirring once every hour or so.
4. Drain liquids from veggies. (Note: Liquid can be saved as broth.)
5. Veggies are done when they are soft.

Cheesy Paleo-Style Tortillas

Prep Time: 10 minutes
Cook Time: 0 hours, 30 minutes
Total Time: 0 hours, 40 minutes
Servings: 3-5

Ingredients

- 3 tablespoons olive oil
- 2 lbs. ground turkey
- 1 ½ teaspoons salt
- ½ teaspoon black pepper
- 1 packet of natural gluten free cheddar cheese
- 2 sweet peppers, minced
- 1 tomato, minced
- 1 onion, minced
- ½ tablespoon of meat seasoning
- Gluten-free tortillas

Instructions

1. Preheat oven to 390 degrees Fahrenheit
2. In a bowl, mix ground beef with minced tomatoes, onions, and seasoning. Set aside
3. In a skillet, add olive oil and beef.
4. Cook beef over medium heat for 6 minutes.
5. Spray (9x13) foil pan with non-stick spray.
6. Place tortillas in the pan
7. Place meat in each tortilla
8. Add cheese on top
9. Bake for 12 more minutes.

10.   Tortillas are done when they are golden brown.

Lemony Chicken Slow cooker style

Prep Time: 10 minutes
Cook Time: 4 hours, 15 minutes
Total Time: 4 hours, 25 minutes
Servings: 3-5

Ingredients

- 7 large lemons, peeled and sliced
- 1 entire chicken (medium size, 3.5-6 lbs.)
- 2 tablespoons of all-purpose seasoning
- 1 teaspoon salt
- 1 teaspoon black pepper

Instructions

1. Coat inside and outside of chicken in seasoning, salt, and pepper.
2. Spread lemons around and inside the chicken
3. Cook for on high for 4 hours and 15 minutes.
4. Note: Chicken may be done earlier, so check after 3 hours to see if cooked properly
5. After chicken is cooked well done leave in slow cooker and let cool for 10 minutes

Honey Glazed Chicken Wings

Prep Time: 11 minutes
Cook Time: 3 hours, 30 minutes
Total Time: 3 hours, 41 minutes
Servings: 7-10

Ingredients

- 15-25 small chicken wings
- 1 cup natural honey
- 1 tablespoon all-purpose season
- 3 tablespoons olive oil
- ½ teaspoon salt
- ½ teaspoon black pepper
- 2 sweet peppers, minced

Instructions

1. Add wings to slow cooker, set aside.
2. In a wide bowl, mix together honey (if the honey is very thick add ¼ cup of hot water), olive oil, sweet peppers, salt, and black pepper
3. Spread mixture evenly over the chicken wings
4. Cook on medium heat for 3 ½ hours

Honey Glazed Drumstick Medley

Prep Time: 10 minutes
Cook Time: 4 hours, 30 minutes
Total Time: 4 hours, 40 minutes
Servings: 7-10

Ingredients

- 7-16 chicken legs (as many as will fit in slow cooker)
- 1 cup natural honey
- 1 tablespoon all-purpose season
- 3 tablespoons olive oil
- ½ teaspoon salt
- ½ teaspoon black pepper

Instructions

1. Add wings to slow cooker, set aside.
2. In a wide bowl, mix together honey (if the honey is very thick add ¼ cup of hot water), olive oil, salt, and black pepper.
3. Spread mixture evenly over the chicken wings.
4. Cook on medium heat for 4 ½ hours.

Sweet Potato Chicken Mash slow cooked

Prep Time: 45 minutes
Cook Time: 4 hours, 30 minutes
Total Time: 5 hours, 15 minutes
Servings: 4-6

Ingredients

- 1 ½ lbs. boneless chicken breasts, cut into bite size pieces
- 3 sweet potatos, peeled and sliced into bite size pieces
- 4 sweet peppers, minced
- 1 tomato, minced
- 1 onion, minced
- ½ tablespoon meat seasoning
- 2 tablespoons olive oil

Instructions

1. In a slow cooker, place in the boneless chicken breast pieces.
2. Add in peeled and cut potatoes.
3. Add in sweet peppers, tomato, seasoning, salt, and pepper..
4. Cook on high heat for 4 ½ hours.
5. Check at 3 ½ hours to see if potatoes are soft and tender (this is a sign that food almost done); if not, continue cooking until done.

Thai Curry Chicken

Prep Time: 11 minutes
Cook Time: 6 hours, 0 minutes
Total Time: 6 hours, 41 minutes
Servings: 7-10

Ingredients

- 7-9 chicken drumsticks
- 1 can of coconut milk
- ½ onion, chopped
- 1" ginger, minced
- 1 sweet pepper, minced
- 1 teaspoon salt
- 1 teaspoon pepper
- 1 ½ tablespoons of curry powder

Instructions

1. Cut around the bottom of each drumstick to sever the tendons, then use a paper towel to remove the skin from chicken.
2. Add chicken and all other ingredients to slow cooker.
3. Cook on low heat for 5-6 hours.

Orange Flavored Chicken Paleo style

Prep Time: 15 minutes
Cook Time: 4 hours, 30 minutes
Total Time: 4 hours, 45 minutes
Servings: 7-10

Ingredients

- 1 ½ lbs. boneless chicken breasts, cut into bite size pieces
- 4 oranges, peeled and sliced
- 2 tablespoons apple cider
- 1 teaspoon salt
- 1 teaspoon black pepper
- 1 tablespoon all-purpose seasoning
- 3 tablespoons olive oil
- Non-stick spray

Instructions

1. In a wide bowl, mix together salt, apple cider, all-purpose seasoning, olive oil, and black pepper.
2. Coat chicken pieces in seasoning mixture.
3. Spread peeled orange around chicken.
4. Place everything in the slow cooker.
5. Cook on high heat for 4 ½ hours (check chicken after 3 hours to see if done).
6. Let chicken cool for 10 minutes.

Sweet Treats

Just because you're following the paleo lifestyle doesn't mean you have to give up tasty, delectable desserts! These paleo-safe treats are sure to satisfy your sweet tooth. Better yet, they'll work with your slow cooker, making them easy to prepare!

Maple Gazed Pecans Slow Cooked

Prep Time: 10 minutes
Cook Time: 3 hours, minute
Total Time: 3 hours, 10 minutes
Serving: 3-5

Ingredients

- 3 cups raw pecans

- ¼ cup maple syrup

- 2 teaspoons ground vanilla beans (vanilla extract can be substituted)

- 1 teaspoon sea salt

- 1 tablespoon coconut oil

Instructions

1.   Throw all ingredients into slow cooker.
2.   Cook on low heat for a 1-3 hours, making sure to stir often.
3.   Store in a mason jar after they have cooled completely.

Stuffed Apple coconut cream slow cooked

Prep time 10 mins
Cook time 3 hours
Total time 3 hours 10 mins

Serves: 4

Ingredients

- 4 green apples, cored, bottom still in place
- ½ cup Coconut Cream Concentrate or homemade coconut butter, melted
- ¼ cup sunbutter, unsweetened (or other nut butter)
- 2 tablespoons cinnamon (or more, to taste)
- pinch of nutmeg
- pinch of salt
- 3-4 tablespoons unsweetened shredded coconut
- 1 cup water

Instructions

1. Mix together coconut butter, sunbutter, cinnamon, nutmeg, and salt.

2. Place cored apples in your crockpot and pour water in the bottom.

3. Use a spoon to pour in your coconut and sun butter mixture into each apple until it's at the top.

4. Top each apple off with cinnamon and shredded coconut.

5.   Cook for 2-3 hours on low heat. (Note: Cook longer for softer apples.)

Conclusion

Congratulations! You now have the tools to embark on, or continue, your paleo lifestyle. We hope you're more confident and excited to take on this incredible journey. With this book, you have everything you need to know about what a paleo lifestyle entails, how to use a slow cooker, and several recipes to get you started. Making a change in your lifestyle can be challenging, but this change will allow you to return to a more simplistic style of eating, one that is nearly innate in each and every one of us.

Good luck!

Free Gift

I want to say Thank You for buying my book so I put together a free gift for you!

"Bonus Recipes to checkout"

This gifts is the perfect compliment to this book so just hit the link below to get access

Click Here to Download Your Free Gift.

Tom Soule Collection

Reference

"What to Eat on The Paleo Diet | Dr. Loren Cordain." *The Paleo Diet*. N.p., n.d. Web. 18 May 2015.

"What Is The Paleo Diet?" *The Paleo Diet Robb Wolf on Paleolithic Nutrition Intermittent Fasting and Fitness*. N.p., 17 Feb. 2012. Web.

"Paleolithic Diet." *Wikipedia*. Wikimedia Foundation, n.d. Web. 18 May 2015.

"Paleo Diet 101 | Paleo Leap." *Paleo Leap Paleo Diet Recipes Tips*. N.p., 24 July 2010. Web.

"Slow Cooker." *Wikipedia*. Wikimedia Foundation, n.d. Web. 18 May 2015.

Rattray, Diana. "The Benefits of Slow Cooker Cooking." N.p., n.d. Web. 18 May 2015.

Rattray, Diana. "About.com: Southern Food." N.p., n.d. Web. 18 May 2015.

"Crockpot Cauliflower Bolognese with Zucchini Noodles." *Inspiralized*. N.p., 14 Apr. 2014. Web.
"Paleo Sausage Stuffed Peppers - PaleoPot - Easy Paleo Recipes - Crock Pot / Slow Cooker / One-Pot." *PaleoPot*

Easy Paleo Recipes Crock Pot Slow Cooker OnePot. N.p., 10 Oct. 2012. Web.

"Slow Cooker Beef Stroganoff." *Balancing Paleo.* N.p., 01 Sept. 2014. Web.

"Crockpot Sugar Detox Dessert Stuffed Apples." *PaleOMG Paleo Recipes RSS.* N.p., n.d. Web. 18 May 2015.

"Paleo Slow Cooker N'Oatmeal - Rubies & Radishes." *Rubies Radishes.* N.p., 05 Nov. 2014. Web.

38787866R00028

Printed in Great Britain
by Amazon